Ten Key Passages from the Bible

PSALM 23.6

Bible Basics for Adults

by Julie B. Sevig

Leader Guide

Augsburg Fortress, Minneapolis

Contents

BIBLE BASICS FOR ADULTS
Ten Key Passages from the Bible Leader Guide
This leader guide has a corresponding learner book.

Editors: Beth Ann Gaede and Carolyn F. Lystig
Designer: Craig P. Claeys
Illustrator: Parrot Graphics/Patti Isaacs

Unless otherwise noted, scripture quotations are from New Revised Standard Version Bible, copyright 1989 Division of Christian Education of the National Council of the Churches of Christ in the United States of America. Used by permission.

Copyright © 1996 Augsburg Fortress
All rights reserved. May not be reproduced with the exception of the materials on pages 24-30.

ISBN 0-8066-2330-6

Manufactured in U.S.A.

3 4 5 6 7 8 9 0 1 2 3 4 5 6 7 8 9

Cover photo: © Lars Hansen Photography

Overview

FEWER AND FEWER ADULTS feel comfortable studying the Bible alone or with others. **Bible Basics for Adults** resources address the needs of adults who may not know basic Bible stories or the importance of the Bible for daily Christian living. These four courses will make it easy for adults who know little about the Bible to study it.

General Objectives

The objectives of these courses are to help learners who are not familiar with the Bible and its stories to:
- gain familiarity with the Bible;
- see the Bible as important to their lives;
- gain confidence in using the Bible for their growth in faith and life;
- see their life stories—their joys, sorrows, relationships, and search for meaning—as part of the larger narrative of the people of God that is presented in the Bible.

Course Descriptions

The four courses and their descriptions are as follows:

1. Ten Key Events in Jesus' Life. This course helps adult learners gain a basic understanding of the life and ministry of Jesus. The central story of God's love is presented through the life, death, and resurrection of God's Son. The six sessions help adult learners connect their life stories with the biblical story of the identity and ministry of Jesus, to see in the life of Jesus and his disciples a connection between the Bible and the concerns and hopes of the contemporary world.

2. Ten Key People from the Bible. Adults are introduced to stories of important biblical characters. In this course, adult learners not only enjoy the study of the Bible through stories, but see in those accounts questions and issues that connect with their own lives and journey of faith today.

3. Ten Key Events from the Bible. While this study identifies the life, death, and resurrection of Jesus as the pivotal event of history and the source of our meaning and hope, God's surprising and compassionate deeds help the learner to see that God's creative power has been at work throughout history and is still at work in our journey of faith today.

4. Ten Key Passages from the Bible. This course presents biblical themes that are central to the Christian faith. Through this study participants will celebrate the Christian message in both the Old and New Testament. Living in a world often fraught with fears and disappointments, adults will be encouraged with the life of faith that is filled with prayer, praise, and thanksgiving.

Using the Leader Guide

LEADERS of the **Bible Basics for Adults** courses will discover a helpful new approach awaiting them as they explore each leader guide. Leaders will teach from a two-page session plan designed to allow easy access to ideas for each segment of class time.

Introductions. Each leader guide begins with these introductory resources:
- a description of the adult learner;
- help for using the leader guide to integrate the learners' life experiences in basic Bible study;
- a course introduction.

Session plans. Each two-page session plan begins with a theme statement that highlights a basic biblical concept shared by the session's two biblical texts.

The first five session plans follow this format:
- **Gathering.** An idea for community building and introducing the session theme;
- **Read the Story.** A strategy for reading the first Bible text of the session;
- **Expand the Story.** Ways to discover what the text says about God, the people of God, and the learners;
- **Read the Story.** A strategy for reading the second Bible text of the session;
- **Expand the Story.** Ways to discover what the text says about God, the people of God, and the learners;
- **Focus the Stories.** Activities that focus on the connections learners are able to make between their lives and the two featured Bible texts.

The sixth session plan follows a similar format but focuses on one biblical text. Leaders will choose activities from each part of the session that best meet the needs of the learners. To prepare for an activity listed on a session plan, a leader may be directed to another page in the guide for the following helps:

Discussion strategies. Ways to involve all learners in actively identifying, sharing, and scrutinizing their opinions and life experiences.

Reproducible pages. Ways to expand, not replace, the activities in the learner book. These include process helps that the learner book cannot accommodate. They are referred to in specific session plans and need to be reproduced before the session for use during or after each session.

Common Resources

All four Bible Basics for Adults courses contain a number of pages that can be copied, distributed, and discussed throughout any of the courses. Or this material may be copied and distributed for the learners' reading enjoyment.

LEARNER BOOK

- **How the Bible Is Organized (page 23).** This outline will help learners identify Old and New Testament books and locate biblical texts more easily for reading and study.
- **Bible Time Line (pages 24-25).** The time line helps learners put the Bible texts they are studying in each course into the larger context of God's salvation story as documented by Scripture. As you begin the study of each text, refer the learners to the time line to help them appreciate the scope and sequence of God at work in the lives of God's people.
- **How to Read the Bible (page 26).** This page provides three tools for beginning Bible readers. "Finding a Bible Reference" shows learners how to interpret a reference and then track down the passage in the Bible. "Going Deeper" provides questions to help learners dig into and apply a text. Bible readers who want to keep notes in their Bibles about their discoveries and questions will find "Marking Your Bible" useful.
- **Glossary (inside back cover).** The glossary in each course defines key words and phrases in that course, and it is placed in the learner book so it is always available to learners. Note that

glossary entries pertinent to each session are identified in a prominent place on each session plan in this guide. Make sure learners understand these words and phrases before the end of each session.

LEADER GUIDE

- **How the Bible Came to Be (page 25).** Learners may begin to ask questions about how the Bible as we know it came to be, and the opportunity to discuss the variety of translations available to us will certainly arise simply because the learners have brought a variety of translations to class. Copy and distribute this page to guide your discussion.
- **Bible Study Resources (page 26).** All of us have questions about what we read in the Bible. This reproducible page provides a brief description of the various types of references, including the study Bible, cross-reference, commentary, handbook, dictionary, and atlas. Particularly helpful is the explanation of how to use a concordance.
- **Bible Bookmarks (page 27).** Copy this reproducible page and cut out markers to help give learners quick access to the key texts being studied. The prayers and hymn texts on the bookmarks can also be used for reflection and prayer at various times between sessions. This serves as a way to connect biblical learning with one's daily life. During the first session, explore with the learners how these bookmarks can be used.
- **Old and New Testament Maps (pages 28-29).** These reproducible maps help learners find important biblical locations in relationship to the Middle East today. Old and New Testament sites are identified on page 29. Make copies of these maps for each learner and refer to the maps at appropriate times during the sessions.
- **The Bible in Worship (page 30).** The Bible is at the center of Christian worship. From the Bible comes much of the content and the general form of our worship. This reproducible page discusses liturgy as the pattern of Bible texts we hear, sing, and pray in worship.
- **Using these Resources in Other Settings (page 31).** Because of the diverse schedules and interests of adult learners, other ways to use this resource are explored. Consider using these other settings as ways to reach more people with this and other Bible studies.

About the Learner

THESE RESOURCES ARE DESIGNED for adults who have an interest in learning basic Bible stories and exploring the importance of the Bible in daily Christian living. Researchers suggest that three quarters of adults in the church do not participate in Bible study. Add to this the number of adults joining churches, and the potential audience for basic Bible study is tremendous. Providing the opportunity to help adult learners become familiar with Bible stories, and to gain confidence in their ability to read and understand Scripture, to grow in faith, and to address the issues they face in their lives is a priority for church education leaders.

Getting Started

Adults choose to participate in Bible study groups for a variety of reasons. Research indicates that the following are important factors to consider as you establish Bible study groups in your church.

Adults participate when they believe the experience will help them grow in a way that will benefit them, their families, and their communities. Adults are motivated to finds ways to "make life work" as they face the challenges of daily living. Issues that arise from relationships, family, aging, job transitions, money, and a variety of circumstances as defined by the learners need to be addressed in Bible study groups.

Adults participate when they are sure they will not be embarrassed by their lack of biblical knowledge or insight. Many Bible study resources and leaders assume a level of familiarity with the Bible and biblical scholarship that most adults find overwhelming and disconnected from the issues of daily life. Walter Wink, a professor of biblical interpretation, suggests that adults seek insight and not just information. It is the intersection of the biblical text with the experience of the learner that evokes insight. Because we are all experts when it comes to our own experience, no one should be made to feel inadequate when it comes to studying the Bible (Walter Wink, *Transforming Bible Study: A Leader's Guide,* 2nd ed. [Nashville, Tenn: Abingdon Press, 1989], 37-38).

Adults participate when they are comfortable with the other learners in the group. Adults know that they will benefit from the opportunity to see and hear what life looks like from the perspective of others. They know that learning comes from asking, sharing, doing, and imagining. But the idea of sharing personal information with strangers can be a barrier to participation. Learners who have not participated in Bible study as adults are more likely to accept an invitation to join a group of people they know or who have similar concerns (for example, parents with teenagers) than they are to sign up for a group in response to an announcement in a bulletin or newsletter.

Adults participate when the time commitment honors their priorities. Finding a time to meet can be a difficult hurdle to overcome. Parents with young children may appreciate a group that meets every other Monday night rather than weekly. This allows them to be with their children and helps with finding child care. A group of older adults may prefer to meet during the day so they do not have to travel at night.

Recruiting

Keep the following suggestions in mind as you establish groups for basic Bible study:

Keep the groups small. This study focuses on the intersection between basic Bible texts and the learner's life experience. A group of 6 to 10 participants allows for a balance of individual reflection and group discussion that is important in this study.

Start with the groups that already exist in your church (parents with young children, new members, empty nesters, Sunday school teachers, young adults, and so on). People who share concerns and situations in life will be more comfortable together and may have similar schedules.

Make personal invitations. Announcements during worship, in bulletins or newsletters, and community papers are important. But many more adults will respond to a personal invitation to participate in a Bible study group. Make sure they know the details of the study, who else will be there, and the expectations of the participants.

Consider allowing the group to decide on the time and meeting place for the study.

Communicate clearly that this is a study for adults who are interested in learning basic Bible stories and exploring the importance of the Bible in daily Christian living. It is important for this audience to know that you respect their experience in life, their ability to read and understand Bible stories, and their interest in making a positive difference in their lives. It is also important for them to know that you do not expect them to be biblical scholars.

Working with the Adult Learner

Adult learners bring a variety of learning styles, experiences, gifts, and questions to the Bible study. Everyone in the group, both learners and leader, has something to offer to other individuals and to the group. It is important for the leader to recognize and respect the diversity of experience and opinion that exists in a group of adult learners. There will not always be agreement or consensus. The leader may find that living with the questions is more important than finding the right answers. Helping the learner to search for better questions and share personal insights is often more productive than looking for answers.

As beginners in adult Bible study, the learners also bring many insecurities and uncertainties about their ability to participate successfully. The questions and activities in the resource help learners explore the biblical material as it connects with their experiences. One of the goals of this course is to help learners become more confident in their ability to read and understand the Bible. Most adults who participate in this basic Bible course will quickly gain the skills and confidence necessary to participate in a more in-depth level of study as they seek to learn how to respond to their call to follow Jesus.

Needs of adult learners

Adults are motivated to participate in Bible study by a diverse set of interests and questions. Kent Johnson, a professor of Christian education, suggests that coping with transitions is the single most common motivating factor (*Developing Skills for Teaching Adults,* Teaching the Faith Participant Guide [Minneapolis: Augsburg Fortress, 1993], 6f). Adults are all, however, seeking enrichment, growth, and ways to make a positive difference in their lives and the lives of others.

Leaders need to recognize the varying needs of the adult learners in their groups. Michael Sack identifies four distinct adult audiences in our churches today. Each generation, according to Sack, has its own identity and needs:

Generation X includes adults who are 16 to 25 years old. They battle low self-esteem and gather in small groups of their peers for support and nurture. They turn to the church for unconditional acceptance and to hear a message of hope.

Busters are 25 to 35 years old. They are firmly grounded and can provide strong leadership for the church. They need relationships, to talk things over with their peers, and to work for a better world.

Boomers are 35 to 50 years old. They look to faith in Christ for a stabilizing influence. They need to discuss meaning, self-definition, and worth.

Older adults are 50 and up. They possess skills and want to do something worthwhile. They need to be appreciated for their experience, insight, and abilities.

This is one way to demonstrate the diversity among adult learners. It is important to recognize that within each of these groups there are individuals who struggle with personal issues. In the course of this study, each individual needs to be heard, respected, and affirmed.

(From *Brain Scan of America* by Michael Sack, copyright © 1995 Michael C. Sack, Cultural Insights, Inc.)

Learning styles

Adult learners have different learning styles. This has to do with how they prefer to encounter and act upon new insights and information. Some adults sit quietly, watching and listening to the group before drawing their own conclusions. Others appreciate the opportunity to do a skit or play a role to express their thoughts and feelings. Some prefer a presentation followed by a question-and-answer period. Others show little interest in group solutions, preferring to act as individuals on practical problems.

To help the leader accommodate the various learning styles of the adult learner, this resource presents two biblical texts—brief segments in the learner book that put the texts into their biblical context—and activities that encourage learning through asking, telling, doing, and imagining. The leader should select activities that guide the participants in a dialogue with the text at all levels—thinking, feeling, intuition, and experience.

Course Introduction

IN THIS COURSE, *Ten Key Passages from the Bible*, learners study important passages that guided our ancestors and speak to us as well. They will learn about God's love for them and be empowered for service to their neighbors.

1. Commandments Given in Love. The learners discover that God gave the law and the promise of salvation to the Israelites and to all of God's people.

2. Walking the Walk. The learners discover that God, who never leaves us, calls us to work for justice.

3. Created in Love that Does Not End. This session focuses on God's love for us in Christ Jesus, which makes us a new creation.

4. Grace and Grace Alone. This session reminds the learners that we are saved by grace through faith in Christ Jesus.

5. For God So Loved the World, Forever. The learners are reminded of God's great love for us and God's promise that we will live together, forever.

6. Rejoicing in God's Favor. In this session, we offer joyful praise and thanksgiving to God, whose favor is for a lifetime.

Each session is divided into two parts: "Expand the Story" and "Focus the Stories." An "Expand the Story" section appears twice—once for each of the two texts in each session. ("Expand the Story" only appears once in the last session because the focus of this session is on reviewing the 10 key passages from the previous sessions, not on exploring a new text.) The section helps both learner and leader put the passage in its biblical context.

"Expand the Story" gives information about the book of the Bible from which the passage comes, and in some cases, about the book's writer. In the sessions focusing on passages from Paul's letters, "Expand the Story" sheds light on the people to whom he wrote.

The "Focus the Stories" section helps learners apply the text to their life. Through activities and discussion, learners connect the passage to their life and look with other learners for its meaning. Both "Expand the Story" and "Focus the Stories" help the learner to answer three important questions:
- What do the texts tell me about God?
- What do the texts tell me about the people of God?
- What do the texts say about me?

It is around these three questions that the learner is taught to read and study these key passages. The hope of this course is that learners will be inspired to continue study in God's Word and service to others. You, the leader, have the privilege of empowering them to do so and seeing what surprises might surface.

Course Objectives

This course will help the learners:
- learn basic Bible passages about the saving activities of God;
- recognize the Bible as God's living Word that reveals God's love and grace for all;
- respond to God's living Word with praise, thanksgiving, and service to others.

1 Commandments Given in Love

God gave the law and the promise of salvation to the Israelites and to all of God's people.

Deuteronomy 6:4-9   Hear, O Israel
Exodus 20:1-17   The Ten Commandments

Gathering

☐ Take all the hearts from a deck of cards and ask each learner to draw one from you. Have each person introduce himself or herself and list people or activities they love—as many as the number on their card indicates.

● ● ● ● ● ● ● ● ● ● ● ● ● ● ● ● ● ● ● ●

Deuteronomy 6:4-9
Hear, O Israel

Read the Story

☐ Point out that Deuteronomy is the fifth book in the Old Testament. Ask several people who are comfortable reading aloud to read one or two verses each. Or have one person read the entire text.

Expand the Story

☐ Direct the learners to "Hear, O Israel" (learner book, page 3). Ask those who are willing to read to take turns reading this section aloud. Pronounce *Shema* and *Yahweh* (phonetically spelled in the learner book) for them before beginning.

☐ Ask the learners to look again at the text, especially the first two verses. Can they see how these powerful words could be considered a creed for the Jewish people? What do these words and the words that flow from them say about God? (*God is a jealous God, wanting unwavering devotion and love.*) What does the text say about the people of God? (*They are to make loving God a part of everyday life, teaching the Shema to their children and sharing it with all—evangelism in the broadest sense.*) What does the text say about us? How can these words of faith be personalized? (*Answers will vary.*) (See the discussion strategy "Rewrite" on page 21.)

☐ As was noted in the learner book, Jesus, himself a rabbi, often quoted the Shema in his preaching and teaching. He called it the First, or Great, Commandment. Ask three people to locate (provide direction as needed) and read aloud Jesus' teaching on the Great Commandment in the Gospels: Matthew 22:34-40; Mark 12:28-34; and Luke 10:25-28. Invite comment and discussion on how the versions vary. (See the "Teaching Twosome" strategy on page 21.)

● ● ● ● ● ● ● ● ● ● ● ● ● ● ● ● ● ● ● ●

Exodus 20:1-17
The Ten Commandments

Read the Story

☐ On seven slips of paper, write:
   • Exodus 20:1-3;
   • Exodus 20:4-6;
   • Exodus 20:7;
   • Exodus 20:8-11;
   • Exodus 20:12;
   • Exodus 20:13-16; and
   • Exodus 20:17.
Distribute the slips to people who are willing to read. As they read the verses in order, learners can follow along in their Bibles. As appropriate, identify and talk about potential differences in meaning presented by variations in Bible translations.

Expand the Story

☐ Ask the learners to comment on the Ten Commandments. What do they think of when they hear them? What images come to mind? What have they heard or learned in the past about the Ten Commandments? (See the strategy "Orbit" on page 20.)

- [ ] Direct them to "The Ten Commandments" in their learner books (page 6) and invite them to follow along while you read aloud. When you have finished reading, reinforce some of the key points about this text: 1) Moses received the Ten Commandments on behalf of the people of Israel, whom God had delivered from slavery; 2) the Commandments were given in love, to protect us and shape our life together; and 3) the Commandments are law, not gospel. They do not save. Christ saves, which is why we call him the fulfillment of the law.

- [ ] Note that the Commandments, although originally carved in stone, are not inexhaustible. Many contemporary evils and ethical issues are not covered and were not anticipated by the Commandments. Given the opportunity, in fact, we probably would like to add some of our own. Whatever our circumstances or dilemmas, we consider the Commandments a starting point in our struggle to live together in peace.

- [ ] Prepare a list of modern dilemmas and propose which commandment might address each situation. Use the strategy "Roll Call" (page 20) to elicit learners' views about whether the Commandments do indeed provide guidance for resolving the dilemma.

- [ ] Encourage the learners to comment on the text and on what they've read in the learner book. See the strategy "Who's Ready?" on page 21.

•••••••••••••••••••••••

Focus the Stories

Depending on the needs and personalities of your group's members, use one of the following activities to help learners see how the two texts relate to this session's focus.

- [ ] Form groups of three or four people. Write one number, 1 through 10, on slips of paper.

  Tell the learners each small group is going to interpret a commandment for the large group. Each group should draw a number of a commandment and "sculpt" the members of the group in such a way that the others might guess which commandment they are sculpting. This is a silent activity, with group members arranging themselves or each other.

  Make your way around the room, giving needed ideas or assistance. Allow yourself to be recruited for groups that need an additional sculpture ele-

ment. Encourage them to be creative and to use props that might be in the room. Allow them time to plan their sculpting before presenting it for the other groups, and tell other groups not to start guessing until the human sculpture is still and silent.

After they have had some fun presenting their human sculptures, gather the group together to form one more sculpture: the Shema. Encourage teamwork and try to involve everyone in the final product.

Spend some time debriefing the exercise by eliciting their comments. How did they feel about doing the exercise? What did they learn from the experience—about the text, or about themselves or others?

- [ ] If you are working with a smaller group of learners or you think your group would not be comfortable with the sculpting exercise, proceed as above but ask learners to interpret the commandment by drawing a picture.

- [ ] Ask learners to form groups of three or four people (or ask them to stay in their sculpting/drawing groups), and direct their attention to "Focus the Stories" (learner book, page 9). Allow them several minutes to read the section and reflect on it. Then ask them to share their insights with one another in their small groups. (See "A Moment of Solitude," page 23.)

Closing

- [ ] Return to the large group for comments and closing. Ask the learners what was meaningful about this session for them and what they will take home with them. (See "The Great Place," page 22.)

- [ ] Close by reading Deuteronomy 6:4-9 and Matthew 22:34-40. Invite someone to read aloud the prayer on page 10 in the learner book.

② Walking the Walk

God, who never leaves us, calls us to work for justice.

Micah 6:8 Do Justice
Psalm 23:1-6 The Divine Shepherd

Gathering

☐ Invite learners to introduce themselves, and give them each two to three minutes to tell about a "scary walk" they've had, as either a child or an adult. What happened, and who was there to comfort them?

• •

Micah 6:8
Do Justice

Read the Story

☐ Point out that verse 8 is really a response to the verses immediately before it. Ask three people to read, the first person reading Micah 6:1-5; the second one, Micah 6:6-7; the third person, Micah 6:8.

Expand the Story

☐ Ask the learners to find the section "Do Justice" (learner book, page 11). Invite them to take turns reading it aloud, one paragraph each.

☐ Call attention to the portion in the learner book that compares the Micah text to a temple entrance liturgy. Ask two people to find Psalm 15:1-2 in their Bibles, and two others to locate Psalm 24:3-4a. (Point out that *a* is the first part of the verse).

☐ Tell them a worshiper at a temple gate might say the words of Psalm 15:1 (ask someone to read this aloud) and that a priest would answer (have someone read Psalm 15:2). Or a worshiper might ask (have Psalm 24:3 read) and receive the answer (verse 4a: "those who have clean hands and pure hearts").

☐ Direct the learners back to the Micah 6:8, and ask whether they have questions or comments.

☐ Ask: What does the text tell us about God? *(Answers will vary, but the learner book has already indicated that God wants only "us"—people who work for justice, love one another, and walk with God.)*

☐ Ask: What does this text say about God's people? *(Like the pilgrim, we yearn to be put right with God. We might think we can obtain this by concentrating only on our relationships with God. Instead, we are instructed to live with God and for others, especially for the oppressed.)*

☐ If any group members are willing to personalize the text by saying what it means to them, encourage them to do so. You might set the stage by using the strategy "Tell It Like It Is" on page 23.

• •

Psalm 23:1-6
The Divine Shepherd

Read the Story

☐ Divide the group in two and ask them to read Psalm 23 antiphonally. The first group can read the odd numbered verses; the second group, the even numbered verses.

Expand the Story

- [ ] Ask the learners whether Psalm 23 is familiar to them. If so, in what instances have they read it or heard it read? Allow time for discussion. (Because many people have had important personal experiences involving this psalm, the strategy "Focus on Feelings," page 20, might be appropriate.)

- [ ] Direct them to "The Divine Shepherd" (learner book, page 14) and allow them time to read it silently. Ask whether they have questions and whether they would like to discuss further anything they read in this section. Use the strategy "Go with What's Hot," page 21.

- [ ] Be prepared to explain the different types of psalms and to give examples of each: thanksgiving and praise (Psalms 66; 103); lament (Psalm 79); trust (Psalm 121); confession (Psalm 51); history and creation (Psalm 104); wisdom (Psalm 15); royal and enthronement (Psalm 110).

- [ ] Point out the intimacy of Psalm 23. Although the image of God as shepherd was common to the people of Israel, what makes this psalm so powerful is the intimate relationship between the shepherd and one person: "I." That intimacy is portrayed in the New Testament as well, evidenced by the many references to Jesus as the shepherd.

- [ ] Ask three people to locate and read aloud these shepherd references: Luke 15:3-6 (the parable of the lost sheep); John 10:11 (Jesus, the good shepherd); and 1 Peter 2:25 and 5:4 (Jesus, guardian of souls, chief shepherd).

- [ ] Using the strategy "Alpha and Omega," page 20, invite learners to look at Psalm 23 again with this study's defining questions in mind: What does the psalm tell us about God? *(God gives all we need, guides our life, doesn't leave us, promises eternal life.)* What does the psalm say about the people of God, and about us in particular? *(We need those things that God provides, as well as comfort and mercy; answers will vary.)*

• •

Focus the Stories

Depending on the needs and personalities of your group's members, use one of the following activities to help learners see how the two texts relate to this session's focus.

- [ ] For this exercise, you'll need a stack of newspapers. Form groups of three or four and assign each group a theme: doing justice, loving kindness, walking humbly. Ask each group to find a gathering space away from the others and give each group several newspapers. Ask the groups to look for situations in which applying the focus of their group might have changed a situation. For example, a report about someone suffering from poverty might end differently if justice (equity) were really available for all people. Or maybe they will find a story in which justice, love, or a humble walk was present.

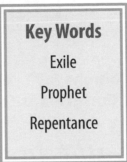

Key Words

Exile

Prophet

Repentance

  Offer extra credit for happy endings. Discourage them from being judgmental. Ask them to look instead for events that would be changed if we took seriously Micah's words of wisdom. When they've finished, allow them a few minutes to report their findings to the other groups.

- [ ] Direct learners to "Focus the Stories" (learner book, page 16). Ask them to skim Psalm 23 and to select one verse that seems to speak to them. Ask learners to read the reflection question for that verse in the learner book, and to write a few sentences in response to that question. Invite them to pair off with another person to discuss their reflections. When you've allowed enough time for pairs to discuss, call the group back and invite those willing to share their responses to do so. Get feedback on what discoveries they may have made about Psalm 23 and their own lives.

Closing

- [ ] Read Psalm 150 responsively and then offer this prayer or one of your own:

    God of greatness, we thank you for our time together, our learning, and this community of faith. In our world of brokenness and pain, help us to be instruments of peace and justice. And when we are burdened with injustice, oppression, and broken and strained relationships, remind us again and again of your love and promises. Amen.

③ Created in Love that Does Not End

God's love for us in Christ Jesus makes us a new creation.

Romans 8:31-39 God's Love in Christ Jesus
2 Corinthians 5:17-21 A New Creation

Gathering

☐ Ask learners to introduce themselves by saying their name and briefly telling of a time they were separated from their parents—perhaps when they got lost or were away from home for the first time.

● ●

Romans 8:31-39
God's Love in Christ Jesus

Read the Story

☐ Tell learners that the first story for this session reminds us that nothing separates us from God. Ask one person to read aloud Romans 8:31-35 and a second person to read Romans 8:36-39

Expand the Story

☐ Have learners locate on the map in the learner book (page 20) the city of Rome, to which this letter from Paul was sent, as well as Corinth, the city where he probably wrote. Christians in Corinth received the letter containing the second text for this session.

☐ Ask learners whether the passage is familiar. Tell them it is often used as a funeral text, and ask why it might be chosen for funerals. (*It is filled with God's promise to save us; comforting words that say nothing—even death—can separate us from the love of God.*)

☐ Invite learners to take turns reading aloud a paragraph each from "God's Love in Christ Jesus" (learner book, page 19). When they've finished, ask for comments or questions. (See the strategy "Orbit" on page 20. Encourage learners to connect the text to their own experience.)

☐ Ask what the passage says about God. (*God is for us, and gave God's only Son, who goes before God and "pleads our case"—that we belong to God because of what Christ Jesus has done for us.*) What does the passage tell us about God's people? (*We're vulnerable to brokenness but comforted by God's promises.*)

☐ To personalize the text, ask learners what seems to separate us from God. (*They may list those things in Romans 8:37-39, and add others of their own.*) As they list them, write the items they mention on a white board, chalkboard, or large sheet of paper.

☐ Ask learners to spend a moment looking at the list, and remind them that God's love is greater than all that has been listed. These words from Paul are words of promise and comfort—to the Romans and to us as well.

● ●

2 Corinthians 5:17-21
A New Creation

Read the Story

☐ Paul gives a passionate plea to the people of Corinth. Read the verses aloud to the learners and ask them to follow along, underlining words that are meaningful to them. (Note and discuss differences in Bible translations as appropriate.)

Expand the Story

☐ After having spent considerable time in Corinth, Paul was saddened to hear about division in the church there. This letter, and particularly this passage, is a plea for the Corinthians to listen to the good news of Christ.

☐ Define *reconciliation*. Ask for ideas about what it means and offer some of your own. *(Reconciliation speaks of forgiveness, of being restored into a relationship. For Christians, Christ's death and resurrection "reconciles" us to God.)*

☐ Ask one person to read "A New Creation," and ask learners to comment on what has been read. (See the strategy "Rewrite" on page 21.)

☐ Remind learners that this passage is another radical sermon by the apostle Paul. Imagine what people of that time must have thought about this "new creation." Remember the popular children's toys called "transformers" (figures that could be completely turned into something else)? Paul's words call us to be "transformed" into a new creation.

☐ Tell learners that to Paul's critics, Paul was a threat. The Greeks emphasized wealth and vocation, even family. It was on those bases that they judged others—and Paul (who some of them considered only a noisy tentmaker). Using the strategy "One-on-One Coverage" (page 20), ask learners to discuss two questions: How do we judge others? What does the passage say to us about our relationships with God and others?

● ●

Focus the Stories

☐ Direct them to "Focus the Stories" in their books (page 29), and ask them to read it silently. That section provides questions to help them begin reflecting on the passages and applying them to their own lives.

☐ Distribute to the learners 8½" x 14" sheets of white paper (legal size) and crayons. Tell them they're going to have the chance to think about what the two texts for this session mean to them.

☐ The Romans text is about God's love for us, which breaks through all that might appear to separate us from God. The 2 Corinthians text is about being "in Christ" and, as a result, being part of a "new creation."

> **Key Words**
> Epistle
> Evangelist
> Grace
> Reconciliation

☐ Some adults are resistant to doing art work because they're afraid they're not "good enough" or because they aren't able to think of what to draw. Assure them that this is an activity of creativity and personal expression. Anything goes, and all art work is acceptable.

☐ Tell them they may draw about either text, but encourage them to personalize the text. Questions in the learner book should guide them, but tell them to use their own imaginations. Be encouraging and upbeat with those who are unsure about drawing.

☐ Break into groups of not more than three people so learners don't feel threatened or aren't embarrassed to share their art. Be aware that some pictures or sharing may be quite personal. Invite them to show the rest of their small group their creations and talk about them.

Closing

☐ Gather the groups together for closing. Say: Sometimes hearing the texts again after discussion and reflection is especially meaningful.

☐ Ask one person to read Romans 8:31-39 and another to read 2 Corinthians 5:17-21.

☐ Hand out copies of the hymn, "Dear Christians, One and All" (see reproducible copy on page 24 of this book.) Close by reciting or singing together stanzas you've selected from the hymn.

④ Grace and Grace Alone

We are saved by grace through faith in Christ Jesus.

Ephesians 2:8-10 By Grace
Hebrews 11:1-3 Through Faith

Gathering

☐ Ask learners to tell about a special gift they've received, either as a child or adult. Be prepared to begin conversation by telling about a gift of your own. Tell them this session is about the free gift of God's grace.

● ●

Ephesians 2:8-10
By Grace

Read the Story

☐ Invite the learners to read Ephesians 2:1-10. Ask one person to read aloud verses 1-3; another, verses 4-7; and a third, verses 8-10. The other learners may listen, which is how the Ephesians would have experienced receiving this letter.

Expand the Story

☐ Using the strategy "Think About It" (page 21), post a large sheet of paper on which you have written the statement: Grace means "no strings attached."

☐ Direct the learners to "By Grace" (learner book, page 31) and ask those who are willing to read a paragraph each.

☐ This epistle is rich in the Christian message of God's grace and promise to create "one holy, catholic, and apostolic church" (Apostles' Creed). Ask learners whether they have questions or comments on the text or the material in the learner book.

☐ Emphasize the "Pauline paradox" in verses 8-10. First, the writer argues passionately that we are saved by grace, not works. But then, good works are encouraged in verse 10. Be sure the learners

understand that all the good works in the world can't put us right with God. But because Christ has already put us right with God, we live as people who have been "recreated" for good works, a response to what God has done.

☐ Discuss the questions posed in the learner book (page 33) about the human struggle to accept grace, our free gift from a loving God. Return to the "Think About It" statement and ask: Why do we resist the idea that "grace" means "no strings attached"? Is it because the world gives a different message, or because it's too good to be true?

● ●

Hebrews 11:1-3
Through Faith

Read the Story

☐ Before reading the Hebrews passage to the group, call to the learners' attention the "Fast Fact" on page 34 about this unusual book of the New Testament. Allow them some time to page through the book of Hebrews.

Expand the Story

☐ Divide the learners into small groups of three or four people. Ask each group to select a recorder, who will write group responses on a piece of paper. Eventually the recorder will write a definition on a large sheet of paper to be seen by the entire group.

- [ ] Invite each group to brainstorm about "faith." (See "Let's Brainstorm" on page 22 for suggestions about this process.) What is faith? How do we know we have faith? How are our lives different because of it? Urge learners to come up with their own small group definition of faith to share with the other groups.

- [ ] Have each group select one or two persons to read aloud "Through Faith" (learner book, page 34). Keeping in mind the Hebrews text, their own definitions and discussions, and the material in the learner book, ask them to focus on these questions: What do we learn about God? What do we learn about God's people?

- [ ] Call the groups back together, and ask each group to share their definitions of faith, as well as their responses to the discussion questions.

- [ ] Use the strategy "One-on-One Coverage" on page 20 to encourage group members to discuss how their lives might be different because of what has just been said. What does all that has been gleaned from this passage say about them, as individuals? When you call the group back together, ask whether anyone is willing to tell what the text means to him or her.

● ●

Focus the Stories

- [ ] Remind the learners that the freeing message of grace is that we can't do anything to earn salvation. There are at least two reasons for this. First, God is perfect, so nothing we could do as sinners can improve on God's perfection. Second, God is love in the purest sense. When we sin against God, we're breaking God's heart. Only God can put us right with God. God has done that through Jesus Christ. The wonderful story of the prodigal son (Luke 15:11-24) helps us visualize God's grace.

- [ ] Direct the learners to "Focus the Stories" (learner book, page 37). Have someone read aloud the introductory comments, and ask another person to read the story from Luke. Or tell them the story of the prodigal son in your own words.

- [ ] Call attention to Luke 15:20, in which the father sees the wayward son while he is still far off. The forgiving father runs to meet him and throws his arms around him, propelled by compassion and love. So it is with God and us.

- [ ] Select one or more of the activities described in the learner book (page 37). Use a discussion strategy appropriate to your group and the activity. Suggestions are prided here. Using the strategy "One at a Time" on page 21, discuss what the story of the prodigal son (or, the forgiving father) says about God and about God's people. *(Answers will vary. God is loving and forgiving; people are sinful and in need of God's grace.)* Ask the learners how they sense God's grace to them. *(Again, answers will vary. Offer these or others of your own: through Word and Sacrament, through the love of another person, by looking at the cross.)*

- [ ] Ask learners to reread Ephesians 2:8-10 and to spend several minutes writing about what it means to be a Christian. Ask learners to share their ideas with one other person. Then ask for volunteers to share their sentences with the whole group.

Key Words
Disciple
Epistle
Faith
Gentiles
Hebrews
Parable
Theology

- [ ] Use the word-association exercise, "Word Piles" (page 23), beginning with the word *faith*. You may want to spend some time discussing how mysterious faith is. In our Western culture, we tend to believe only what we can see. Conclude by reminding learners that it is through our faith that we are saved by grace, and as they have already discovered, that faith is the assurance of things hoped for, and a belief in what cannot be seen.

Closing

- [ ] Close by allowing the learners quiet time to reread the passages for this session. Read or ask for a volunteer to read the prayer in their learner book on page 38.

⑤ For God So Loved the World, Forever

We're reminded of God's great love for us, and God's promise that we will live together, forever.

John 3:16 The Gospel in Miniature
Revelation 1:8 The Alpha and the Omega

Gathering

☐ Invite learners to reflect on and share how they experience God's love and promises. It might be that they sense God's love in worship, in nature, in the love of other people, or in this Bible study group. Set the tone by answering first.

● ● ● ● ● ● ● ● ● ● ● ● ● ● ● ● ● ● ●

John 3:16
The Gospel in Miniature

Read the Story

☐ Divide John 3:16 into as many sections as there are people in your group, and write each section on a piece of 8½" x 11" paper. Hand a sheet to each learner and have them pin or tape the sheets in order to a bulletin board or wall.

Expand the Story

☐ Point out that this verse is often called "the gospel in miniature" because in one sentence, it sums up what God has done for us through Christ.

☐ John 3:16 is perhaps the most famous verse of the Bible, but don't assume all are familiar with it. With that in mind, use the strategy "Word Piles" (page 23), beginning with the word *gave*.

☐ Use the strategy "Tell It Like It Is" (page 23) and talk about a significant experience you or someone else has had with this passage. Encourage learners to describe its meaning for them.

☐ Ask someone to read "The Gospel in Miniature" (learner book, page 39) and invite the group's observations. (See the strategy "Go With What's Hot," page 21.)

☐ To fully appreciate John 3:16, Nicodemus should be introduced (see John 3:1). Nicodemus is the ruler of the Jewish Pharisees, and Jesus takes time to teach him about being born "anew." Although Nicodemus took Jesus literally, Jesus was talking about water and spirit used together to transform a life. If time permits, read all of John 3.

☐ Ask learners what chapter 3 (especially verse 16) says about God *(God is love, God saves and does not condemn);* about the people of God (we are sinful); and about themselves *(answers will vary).*

☐ Remind them that the presence of the Spirit is crucial. Even John 3:16 works to remind us that we are far from God, unless we remember that God does not leave our believing up to us. God promises love first, and grants us the spirit as our helper.

● ● ● ● ● ● ● ● ● ● ● ● ● ● ● ● ● ● ●

Revelation 1:8
The Alpha and the Omega

Read the Story

☐ Direct learners to the last book in the New Testament, the Revelation to John. Ask one person to read verses 1-3 of the first chapter, another to read verses 4-7, and a third to read verse 8. If everyone has the same translation, read verse 8 together.

Expand the Story

☐ Ask learners if they've heard of the book of Revelation and, if so, what images come to mind. Tell them that Revelation has been a misunderstood book, and give several examples of misinterpretations of the book. (For example, some people assert that there will be 144,000 people in heaven, based on Revelation 7:4; others identify contemporary figures, particularly political or religious leaders, as "the beast" in Revelation 11:7.)

Assure them that in spite of some people's misuse of the book, it is still an important book because it points not only to end times but to a faithful God.

☐ Ask learners to locate Rome, as well as the Island of Patmos (off the coast of Ephesus), on their maps (learner book, page 42).

☐ Ask them to take turns reading aloud "The Alpha and the Omega" (learner book, page 42). Making use of the strategy "Go With What's Hot" on page 21, invite them to comment on or ask questions about what they've read. Revelation is a difficult book, but encourage them to look past the confusion and to be comforted by its promises. Although "The Alpha and the Omega" does a good job of explaining what Revelation 1:8 says about God, give learners the opportunity to expand on the ideas in the learner book.

☐ Remind learners that readers of this letter were convinced that the end was near. But in spite of anxiety and fear in a world that seems out of control, God is steadfast and will not abandon us.

☐ Ask learners to spend a few minutes on their own thinking about this question: In our own lives, what does it mean to rely on a God whose love is steadfast? (See "A Moment of Solitude," page 23.) Invite learners to share their thoughts first with a partner and then with the whole group.

● ●

Focus the Stories

☐ Remind learners that in Deuteronomy 6:6-7, the people of God were told to keep the promises of God in their hearts and recite them to their children. Tell them this session's passages of promise lend themselves to memorization. (Indeed, some learners may already know John 3:16 by heart.)

Mention that memorizing Scripture can be most helpful when we are in crisis—that the words are still with us then, even if we feel totally alone. Challenge learners to memorize both verses, but allow those who are resistant or who find memorization difficult to tackle only one.

Key Words

Apocalyptic

Doxology

Gospel

Grace

Litany

☐ If you want to work with your group as a whole, use the strategy "Disappearing Verses" (page 23), to help them memorize these verses.

☐ You might also ask learners to work in pairs. Before they practice with a partner, set the tone by sharing with them John 3:16 and Revelation 1:8 from memory. Then offer these tips:
- Break down a text into parts.
- Picture the action (of the verses) in your mind.
- Memorize entire phrases instead of concentrating on individual words.
- Take your time, and don't be too quick to help your partner when practicing. Pauses are the life rafts of storytellers, even when that "story" is simply a verse.

☐ After learners have had some time to memorize the verses, direct their attention to the questions in the learner book (page 45) that help them to personalize this session's passages. Allow them time in pairs to answer the questions. Tell them that after each person has answered all the questions, his or her partner should share the gospel, using the memorized words from this session.

Closing

☐ Divide your group into two parts, A and Ω. Close by reading the litany (learner book, page 46).

☐ Offer this prayer or one of your own:

Almighty God, we thank you for your promise to be with us always. Thank you for the chance to gather around your Word, to reflect and share, and to be reminded of your promises. We especially thank you for the gift of Christ, who died and rose so that we will live with you forever. In Jesus' name, Amen.

6 Rejoicing in God's Favor

We offer joyful praise and thanksgiving to God, whose favor is for a lifetime.

Psalm 30:4-5 Joy Breaks Like Morning

Gathering

☐ Ask the learners as they gather for this last session to think of a time in their lives when joy followed pain. Set the tone by telling your own story first. (See "Tell It Like It Is," page 23.)

● ● ● ● ● ● ● ● ● ● ● ● ● ● ● ● ● ● ●

Psalm 30:4-5
Joy Breaks Like Morning

Read the Story

☐ Direct learners to the book of Psalms and this session's text, Psalm 30:4-5. Read verses 4 and 5 aloud to them.

Expand the Story

Psalm 30 is a prayer of thanksgiving for deliverance. When we have been helped, we thank the one who helps. That is what Psalm 30 bids us to do.

☐ Allow learners time to read silently all of Psalm 30. After they've finished, ask them what observations they made about God and the people of God. For instance, what images came to their minds? What words are most powerful in this psalm? Which ones carry the most emotion? (See the strategies "Go With What's Hot, page 21; "Focus on Feelings," page 20; and "The Great Place," page 22. Based on your experience with this group, choose the strategy that seems most appropriate.)

☐ Ask someone to read aloud "Joy Breaks Like Morning" (learner book, page 47). Emphasize the psalmist's good news that God's anger and our weeping are short-lived compared to God's favor (which lasts a lifetime) and our joy (which breaks like morning).

☐ Tell learners that although Psalm 30 was written in the first person, it is intended to be a corporate prayer. It has been used throughout the ages by people grateful for God-given changes in their lives. It is used by the community of faith to remember the gift of salvation we find in Christ Jesus.

☐ The psalm is directed at a God who meets our neediness with love and grace. Our response is a life of thanksgiving and praise, assured that God meets our needs, grants us grace, and gives us joy.

● ● ● ● ● ● ● ● ● ● ● ● ● ● ● ● ● ● ●

Focus the Stories

☐ Refer learners to the bookmarks they have received during this course, and spend a few minutes reviewing the Bible passages used for this series. Ask learners what they can recall about each passage, and write a few words about each on a white board, chalkboard, or large sheet of paper. (If you think learners might not have all their bookmarks, reproduce and distribute new sets. See page 27.)

☐ After all the passages are listed, tell learners that through this study they have been challenged to see how their lives—joys, sorrows, relationships, and search for meaning—are part of a larger picture: the story of the people of God through the ages.

- Ask learners to pair off and interview one another. (See "Interviews," page 22, for ideas about how to prepare learners for their interviews.) Encourage them to choose the partner whom they know the least. Direct them to page 48 in the learner book for questions to guide their discussion.

- After the learners have had five minutes to interview their partners (10 minutes total), invite everyone back to the large group. Ask for feedback from the interviews. Caution them to not share anything personal about the person they interviewed without that person's permission.

- Distribute paper to learners and invite them to be creative by writing an acrostic poem using the words of Psalm 30 as a guide. Share this example:

> **People**
> **Rest**
> **Assured**
> **In**
> **God'S**
> **gracE**

- Encourage them to use other words such as JOY, THANKS, and FAVOR. Allow them 10 minutes alone to work on their creations, and then ask each interview pair to share their creations with another pair.

- While they are admiring each other's work, write on a white board, chalkboard, or large sheet of paper this question: Where do I go from here with what I've learned about God, the people of God, and myself? Ask them to answer this question in their groups of four. (Explain the strategy "Orbit," page 20, to guide their discussion.)

- Bring the groups back together for feedback and closing.

Closing

- Refer learners to their bookmarks, and ask for volunteers to locate and read each passages aloud. If a learner has a favorite, encourage him or her to take that slip. (If your group is smaller than 10, ask some people to read more than one passage.)

- After the readings, sing or read together the canticle, "Listen! You Nations" (learner book, page 48), and offer this prayer, "The Prayer of the Church":

  Almighty God, giver of all things, with gladness we give thanks for all your goodness. We bless you for the love which has created and which sustains us from day to day. We praise you for the gift of your Son our Savior, through whom you have made known your will and grace. We thank you for the Holy Spirit, the comforter; for your holy Church; for the means of grace; for the lives of all faithful and good people; and for the hope of the life to come. Help us to treasure in our hearts all that our Lord has done for us, and enable us to show our thankfulness by lives that are wholly given to your service. Amen.

"The Prayer of the Church" reprinted from *Lutheran Book of Worship*, copyright © 1978

Discussion Strategies

Alpha and Omega

Use this strategy to frame a session or topic. Divide the class into pairs. Have each pair discuss an open-ended question designed to elicit the attitudes and ideas of the learners. (For example, if the session is on forgiveness, the questions might include: What is it like to be forgiven by someone? When is it right to forgive?)

Have each pair report to the larger group a condensed version of their responses. Do not follow this with discussion. Go instead to the next activity.

At the end of the session, put the pairs back together to discuss what impact, if any, the session had on them. Did anything from the session make them change their feelings or opinions? Use these answers as a basis for clarification of the session material, further discussion, or other concluding activity.

Roll Call

This activity introduces new material or discussion. Before class, prepare a list of statements that pertain to the material that will be presented. Use statements that state an opinion or fact. Present these statements to the class using an overhead projector or a chalkboard or chart paper. After reading aloud each statement, ask the group to indicate whether they agree, disagree, or want to discuss the statement. Tally the responses and present the results to the group. Follow this activity with discussion.

One-on-One Coverage

From time to time, to vary the discussion format, or when learners are not responding well, ask them simply to turn to one or two others in their vicinity. Everyone has an opportunity to answer the question, and they may or may not report their answers to the large group.

Orbit

Go around the class and ask each person to share one thought, idea, opinion, or outlook on a particular subject. Encourage everyone to explain their answers by referencing a person or experience that shaped the perspective shared.

Focus on Feelings

This strategy is similar to "Go with What's Hot" on the next page. However, while the focus there is on thinking (questions), here the focus is on feeling. Thus, you would ask the learners, "What do you notice you are feeling as we talk about this material?"

This strategy seems to work best when used occasionally. Too much talk about feelings risks silly responses. Too little talk about feelings risks never giving the learners a chance to take the material to heart.

The feeling responses shared by the learners give you a clue about how the material is affecting them. Being empathetic to these feelings can help create an environment of trust and safety in the group. It can also help the learners see that they learn with their feelings as well as their thoughts.

Who's Ready?

In this discussion technique, the learners choose for themselves when to respond. You might say, "Let's discuss these questions. Who would like to begin?"

The advantage of this method is that the learners can talk when they are ready. You, however, will need to make sure each learner responds, and you may have to call on those who don't volunteer.

One at a Time

Call on the learners individually. Direct those not called on to listen quietly and attentively. Ask the learner who is answering to clarify or elaborate as appropriate.

In addition to calling on learners one at a time, you also can ask questions one at a time. That is, have each learner answer the first question, then the second question, and so on.

The advantage of this strategy is that it gives individual attention to each learner and proceeds through the questions in a sequential manner.

Go with What's Hot

The idea here is to focus on the questions that either generate the most enthusiasm or that the learners are most willing to answer. You could say, "Pick one of these questions to answer." The learners then have the freedom to skip questions that are uninteresting to them.

Another option is to ask, "What questions do you have about what we have been reading or discussing?" This strategy allows learners to get at what they want or need to know.

This strategy has the advantage of focusing quickly on what the learners want to talk about. It also can give you clues about what is important to the learners. A disadvantage is that learners might avoid discussing the difficult questions.

(Note: This strategy could be used with the "One at a Time" or "Who's Ready?" strategy.)

Rewrite

Give learners the opportunity to explore the meaning of a specific message or lesson by instructing them to rewrite or tell what they have studied or learned in their own words. Have them work in pairs or small groups. Encourage them to put the information in their own words. Then encourage learners to exchange and discuss what they've written with another pair or small group. Have them find out if what they have written speaks more clearly than the original message. What points did they miss?

Think about It

Although this is not strictly a discussion strategy, at various times in the course ask learners to think about their responses to a question, but do not immediately expect an answer. Simply prepare the question and allow a little silence after you ask it. Defer responses to a time later in the session.

Rather than asking the question aloud, consider printing it in huge letters on newsprint and posting the newsprint where learners can see it during the class. Later, ask the question and encourage learners to respond.

Teaching Twosome

Learners do work on their own; then they find a partner and share with that partner. Next, both learners share with the entire group.

The strategy emphasizes that as learners learn, they also teach, and that we all can learn from each other.

Interviews

Good interviewing skills are basically good communication skills. Use this strategy whenever learners are asked to interview or interact with others about a specific topic.

Interviews can be conducted between two people. They may also be done with a large group interviewing one person. A well-planned interview, carefully thought through by those conducting it, can lead to increased understanding of the experiences of others. It can also be a model for people to see how they might talk about their faith. This strategy will help make the most of opportunities to interview.

1. Begin by asking the people to think about what their goal is for interviewing someone. In general, what do they want to learn or discover? You might ask a group member to be a recorder and write the thoughts of the group on newsprint or a board for everyone to see.

2. Think of as many ways as possible to work towards that goal. Make a list of potential questions and topics. Work together to prioritize what is of highest interest to the group. Then fine-tune the questions or put the topic ideas into question format.

3. If a group will be conducting the interview, decide who is going to ask which questions, giving as many people as possible an opportunity to be involved in interviewing.

4. As you plan your interview and consider the time available, allow for spontaneous interaction, so those doing the interview can respond to what they are hearing and learning.

Let's Brainstorm

Several formats can be used for brainstorming. Learners may begin working individually. Ask them to write the first word, thought, or mental image that comes to their minds related to the issue to be discussed. You may then ask them to share their thoughts within a group of three or four or with the large group. Or in a large group, simply ask learners to offer their ideas aloud, and list all responses on chart paper or a chalkboard.

When brainstorming, remember these guidelines:
- All ideas are accepted.
- Variety is encouraged.
- Ideas are not to be evaluated or ranked.
- Ideas need not be defended.
- A time limit needs to be set.

Brainstorming helps learners gain the confidence that their opinions are valued and do not necessarily have to be backed with lots of facts or align with the opinions of others.

The Great Place

This is a strategy that directs learners in pairs, in small groups, or within the larger group to be affirming of one another when they respond to other learners.

After one learner states an answer or an opinion, the next learner responds by noting one thing that he or she liked about the answer or opinion and then giving his or her own answer. A person might say something like: "You know, that answer really helped me think about things in a different way. I'd never realized that … But I've found that for me …" (Note: You can help teach this method by joining the discussions from time to time and modeling the method.)

Depending on the discussion topic, if you have had learners work in pairs or small groups, allow time for sharing ideas and thoughts with the group as a whole.

Tell It Like It Is

This strategy uses the experiences of the leader to put flesh on the sessions' objectives. It also lets the learners know a little more about you and your faith life. Share a personal story or tell a biblical story in your own words. Try to think of a specific event or story from your own life or the life of someone you know. Students will relate quickly to a personal example.

If you are sharing something about someone else, do not break confidences. The life of a public person might be the source of your example. But if you talk about a friend, relative, or neighbor, use good common sense. Think about the person, situation, and whether it is important to use that material. Then ask the person for permission to tell the story. Decide with the person whether you will change enough facts so that no one in the class could identify the person involved.

Carefully prepare what you will say. Think about important points and write yourself a few notes or outline what you want to express. Don't just "wing it."

Disappearing Verses

Try helping learners memorize a verse by first writing the text on a blackboard and erasing a few words at a time, calling on volunteers each time to recite the entire thing. Finally the verse will disappear, but by that time, most will have it firmly in their mind. Always ask learners to mark it in their Bibles and discuss what meaning it has in daily life.

Word Piles

Play a word association game with the learners. The purpose of this activity is to help you discover what the learners know and think about a topic.

1. Ask learners to list the words or thoughts that come to their minds when you say a word. As they do this, list the words across the top of a chalkboard or chart paper.

2. Underneath each word, ask the learners to add words or pictures that define each of the words they have listed.

A Moment of Solitude

Learners work silently in a corner of the room or in separate areas of the building to master a task, write a report, memorize a piece from the Catechism or Scripture, or write reflections in their journals. Then learners return to group and, if appropriate, share their work. Obviously, this is a somewhat different "discussion" strategy in that sometimes learners discuss a matter not with the group but with themselves or perhaps with God.

The advantage of this strategy is that it cuts down on the distractions that get in the way of learners' work and it helps the learners begin to deal with silent moments in their lives.

Dear Christians, One and All

Martin Luther, 1483–1546;.
tr. Richard Massie, 1800–1887, alt.

Erlich christlich Lieder, *Wittenberg*, 1524

1 Dear Christians, one and all, rejoice, With exultation springing, And, with united heart and voice And holy rapture singing, Proclaim the wonders God has done, How his right arm the vict'ry won, What price our ransom cost him!

2 Fast bound in Satan's chains I lay, Death brooded darkly o'er me, Sin was my torment night and day; In sin my mother bore me. But daily deeper still I fell; My life became a living hell, So firmly sin possessed me.

3 My own good works all came to naught, No grace or merit gaining; Free will against God's judgment fought, Dead to all good remaining. My fears increased till sheer despair Left only death to be my share; The pangs of hell I suffered.

4 But God had seen my wretched state Before the world's foundation, And, mindful of his mercies great, He planned for my salvation. He turned to me a father's heart; He did not choose the easy part, But gave his dearest treasure.

5 God said to his beloved Son:
"'Tis time to have compassion.
Then go, bright jewel of my crown,
And bring to all salvation;
From sin and sorrow set them free;
Slay bitter death for them that they
May live with you forever."

6 The Son obeyed his Father's will,
Was born of virgin mother;
And, God's good pleasure to fulfill,
He came to be my brother.
His royal pow'r disguised he bore,
A servant's form, like mine, he wore,
To lead the devil captive.

7 To me he said: "Stay close to me,
I am your rock and castle.
Your ransom I myself will be;
For you I strive and wrestle;
For I am yours, and you are mine,
And where I am you may remain;
The foe shall not divide us.

8 "Though he will shed my precious blood,
Of life me thus bereaving,
All this I suffer for your good;
Be steadfast and believing.
Life will from death the vict'ry win;
My innocence shall bear your sin;
And you are blest forever.

9 "Now to my Father I depart,
From earth to heav'n ascending,
And, heav'nly wisdom to impart,
The Holy Spirit sending;
In trouble he will comfort you
And teach you always to be true
And into truth shall guide you.

10 "What I on earth have done and taught
Guide all your life and teaching;
So shall the kingdom's work be wrought
And honored in your preaching.
But watch lest foes with base alloy
The heav'nly treasure should destroy;
This final word I leave you."

How the Bible Came to Be

THE OLD TESTAMENT (Jewish Scriptures) was originally written in Hebrew and Aramaic by Hebrew writers. The books of the Old Testament were probably written between 1100 B.C. and 100 B.C. Before being written down, the stories and laws of the Hebrew people were passed on orally from generation to generation.

The New Testament was originally written in Greek. Its authors came from both the Jewish community and the the Greek-speaking Gentile world.

There is considerable agreement that the books known as the Law or Torah (the first five books of the Bible) were the first books to be regarded as Scripture and authoritative. That probably happened about 400 B.C. The other two groups of books in the Old Testament, the Prophets and the Writings, came to be regarded as Scripture later, between 400 B.C. and A.D. 100. Between the third and first centuries B.C., the Jewish Scriptures were translated into Greek for the benefit of Jewish colonists who lived in Greek-speaking areas. This translation was known as the *Septuagint*. The Christian Old Testament canon was formed from it.

In A.D. 98 a council of Jewish scholars at Jamnia established criteria for determining how a book may be considered sacred. Seven books, known as the *Apocrypha,* were rejected by this council. The Protestant Christian churches follow the list of Jewish books as their Old Testament (39 books). They did not accept the Apocryphal books as canonical, or authoritative. The Roman Catholic, Anglican, and Eastern Orthodox churches retain these seven Apocryphal books in their Old Testament for a total of 46 books.

The first Christians, as well as Jesus, used the Jewish Scriptures (Old Testament) as their Bible. Later, between about A.D. 50 and A.D. 124, they wrote their own Scriptures, known as the New Testament. It took nearly three more centuries and many disputes before the present list of 27 New Testament books was adopted as authoritative by the Western church. This list of 27 books was first listed in A.D. 367 in the 39th Festal Letter of Athanasius, a bishop of the church.

Bible Translations

The first Bibles of the Christian community were written in Greek. Later, as Christianity spread to other lands, translations into other languages were needed. The first official translation of the Bible was undertaken by a literary scholar and priest, Jerome, between about A.D. 383 and A.D. 410. Jerome was commissioned by Pope Damascus I to do the authorized Latin version. This translation came to be known as the *Vulgate,* from the Latin word meaning "common" or "everyday." It was the standard version of the Bible for over 1000 years. By the eighth century, only scholars could read and understand Latin. Beginning in the late 14th century, a number of major English translations were completed. Some are described below.

The Wycliffe Bible (A.D. 1384) was the first complete Bible in English. It was translated in secret by John Wycliffe and others from the Latin Vulgate. Copies were written by hand in secret and distributed. Wycliffe was condemned as a heretic because translation of the Latin was forbidden. Some people were burned at the stake for just reading or listening to Wycliffe's translation.

The King James Version (A.D. 1611) was translated by 54 commissioned scholars who based their work on early Hebrew and Greek manuscripts. They gave great attention to style and literary quality. An edition of this Bible was the first English version produced and printed in America.

By the 19th century, many new Greek and Hebrew manuscripts had been discovered, and the English spoken in 1611 had changed greatly. New versions such as the **English Revised** (1885) and the **American Standard** (1901) were created. Later in the 20th century, many more versions were completed. This list of new English and other language translations continues to grow today.

The New Revised Standard Version (A.D. 1989) is the basis for this course. This version is an authorized revision of the Revised Standard Version (1952), which was a revision of the American Standard Version (1901), which embodied earlier revisions of the King James Version (1611).

- When did you hold a Bible for the first time?
- Who put that Bible in your hands?
- Do you know which translation of the Bible that was?
- Where did you get the Bible you are using for this course?
- Which translation of the Bible is it? What do you like about the Bible you are using?
- What questions about your Bible do you have?

Bible Study Resources

AS YOU READ THE BIBLE, expect to have questions about the text. Also know that exploring the Bible can be a daunting job for anyone. But be assured, too, that there are many excellent references to help a person. Here is an overview of the most common types of helps:

Reference materials, short versions of the materials described below, are printed in the backs of some Bibles. The references are often printed as separate volumes, however, and cover topics more extensively.

An **annotated or study Bible** typically contains introductions to the books of the Bible; brief outlines of the books; notes on difficult verses or words; chapter outlines; and articles of general interest on history and geography, translations, and Bible study methods.

The best commentary on the Bible is often a text from another part of the Bible. Therefore, it is often helpful to check the **cross-references**. A cross-reference lists a Bible verse followed by references to one or more related or similar verses. Study Bibles have the most important cross-references listed either in a center column or at the bottom of the page. Cross-references are also known as parallel passages.

A **concordance** helps you locate a Bible passage when you know only a word or phrase from the verse. There are separate concordances for each major translation of the Bible. Find one written for your Bible's translation. To use a concordance, look up a key word from the passage you want to find. Following the word is a list of verses, along with the portion of each passage that includes the key word.

For example, to find the verse that starts "God so loved the world… ," look up the word *world.* Notice that the Bible verses are listed in the order they appear in the Bible. Scan the verses. After John 3:16 you will find the phrase, "God so loved the *w.*" You can look up the passage, explore the surrounding text, and check cross-references.

When you decide which word to look up, choose one that is important in the verse but that is not too common. In this case, for example, you would not look up *God* or *love* because there would be too many references to review easily.

A concordance also helps you do a word study. By checking many references that include the same word, you can explore the way that word is used in the Bible. Often a passage becomes clearer when a key word is understood in a new light.

A **commentary** includes the biblical text plus a verse-by-verse explanation of the Bible. A commentary provides more detail than a study Bible. There are one-volume commentaries on the entire Bible, as well as commentaries with separate volumes for individual books of the Bible.

Handbooks of the Bible do not reprint the text of the Bible, but the articles, which can be extensive, follow the order of the books of the Bible.

A Bible **dictionary** contains short articles on words and topics such as people named in the Bible, groups such as the Pharisees, geography and history, culture, animals, and rituals.

An **atlas** of the Bible, often included in other reference books, provides maps of the Bible lands at various periods of history. You might find helpful a map of Bible lands that prints both the current and ancient names of places.

From *Bible Reading Handbook* by Paul Schuessler, copyright © 1991 Augsburg Fortress.

Bible Bookmarks

Deuteronomy 6:4-9
Hear, O Israel

Prayer for Faithfulness

God of fire and cloud, touch my heart and soul and mind, so that I may be faithful to you. Show me in every moment of my daily walk how to keep your words close to me. In Jesus' name, Amen.

Exodus 20:1-17
The Ten Commandments

A Prayer of Thanks

O Lord, my God, you led the Israelites from slavery into the promised land. Thank you for calling me to be your child and for the gift of your Commandments to protect and guide me. In Jesus' name, Amen.

Micah 6:8
Do Justice

A Prayer for Guidance

Gracious God, I know that your will is that I do justice, love kindness, and walk humbly with you. Be with me and guide me as I strive to do your calling, through the grace of Jesus, the Christ, Amen.

Psalm 23:1-6
The Divine Shepherd

A Table Grace

God of bounty, even on dark and gloomy days, I remember your many gifts to me. Thank you for home and family, for food and clothing, for calling me to serve you, and for your greatest gift of all, your Son, Jesus Christ. Amen.

Romans 8:31-29
God's Love in Christ Jesus

A Prayer for Comfort

Ever present God, you feel so far away, and I need to know that you are with me. Show me your goodness and mercy, and let me feel your comforting touch. In the name of Christ Jesus, our Lord, Amen.

---

2 Cor. 5:17-21
A New Creation

A Prayer for Reconciliation

God of peace, you gave your Son so that we might be reconciled to you. Help me to reach out to those with whom I need to be reconciled, that we may show your love to the world. In Jesus' name, Amen.

Ephesians 2:8-10
By Grace

Amazing Grace

Amazing grace, how sweet the sound, That saved a wretch like me! I once was lost, but now am found; Was blind, but now I see.

John Newton, 1725-1807

Hebrews 11:1-3
Through Faith

A Prayer for Faith

O love who will not let me go, God of Abraham and Sarah, of those who weep and those who rejoice, give me eyes to see your promises at work in my life. For the sake of Jesus, your Son, Amen.

John 3:16
The Gospel in Miniature

Jesus, My Hope

My hope is built on nothing less Than Jesus' blood and righteousness; No merit of my own I claim, But wholly lean on Jesus' name. On Christ, the solid rock, I stand; All other ground is sinking sand.

Edward Mote, 1797-1874, alt.

Revelation 1:8
The Alpha and the Omega

A Prayer for the Close of the Day

Almighty God, you are always with me, when I work and when I play, when I wake and when I sleep. Watch over those I love, and let me slumber this night in your loving arms. In Jesus' name, Amen.

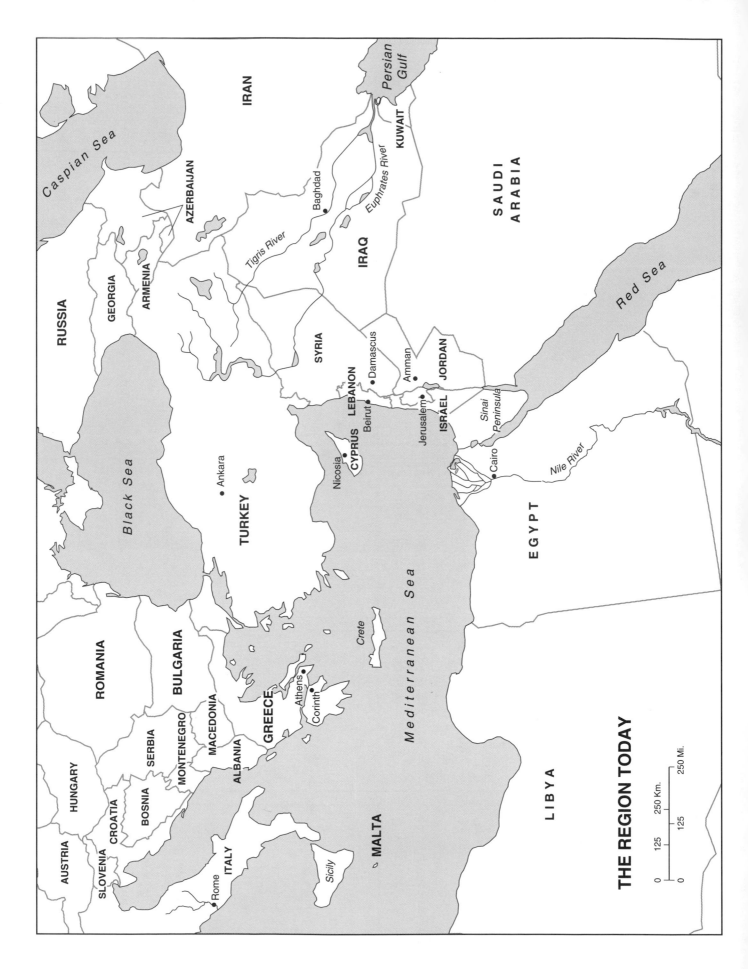

THE REGION TODAY

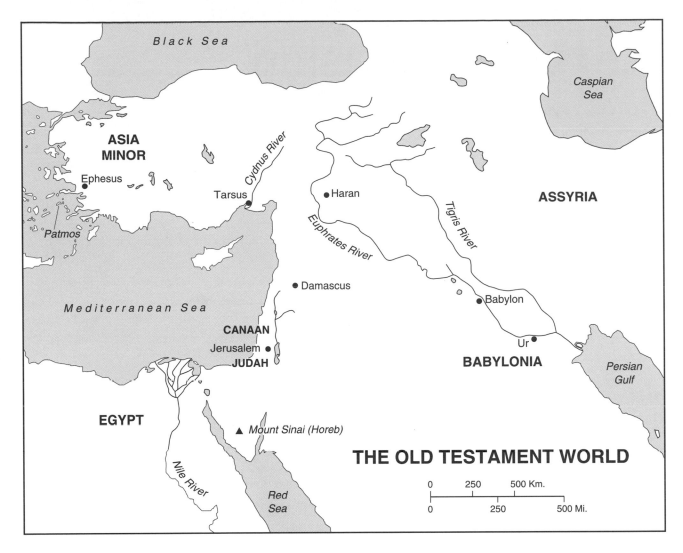

THE OLD TESTAMENT WORLD

Black Sea

Caspian Sea

ASIA MINOR

Ephesus

Tarsus

Cydnus River

Patmos

Haran

ASSYRIA

Euphrates River

Tigris River

Mediterranean Sea

Damascus

Babylon

CANAAN

Jerusalem

JUDAH

Ur

BABYLONIA

Persian Gulf

EGYPT

▲ Mount Sinai (Horeb)

Nile River

Red Sea

0   250   500 Km.

0   250   500 Mi.

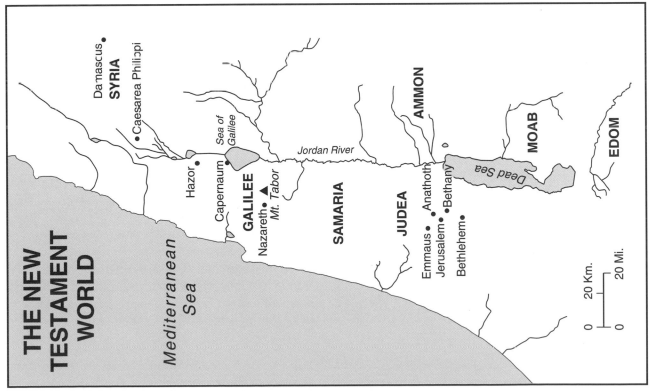

THE NEW TESTAMENT WORLD

Damascus

SYRIA

Caesarea Philippi

Sea of Galilee

Jordan River

AMMON

MOAB

EDOM

Hazor

Capernaum

GALILEE

▲ Mt. Tabor

Nazareth

SAMARIA

JUDEA

Anathoth

Bethany

Dead Sea

Emmaus

Jerusalem

Bethlehem

Mediterranean Sea

20 Km.

20 Mi.

0   0

The Bible in Worship

THE BIBLE IS AT THE CENTER of Christian worship. From the Bible comes much of the content and the general form of our worship. Each Sunday, for example, as many as three different "lessons" or "readings" are used.

In most mainline Christian congregations, the lessons follow a schedule of Bible readings, called the lectionary, that is repeated every three years. The lectionary, in turn, follows the church year, which begins by preparing us for the birth of Christ; continues with a focus on his suffering, death, and resurrection; and ends with an overview of Jesus' teachings.

All the readings reflect the theme for the Sunday's worship. The sermon, hymns, prayers, and other elements of the service further illuminate the central message.

The First Lesson is usually from the Old Testament, and the main point of the lesson is usually parallel to the main point of the Gospel lesson (see below). Often the congregation responds to this lesson by singing (or reading) a psalm, an ancient Hebrew hymn that was first used in worship in Old Testament times.

The Second Lesson is from one of the New Testament letters, the Book of Hebrews, or the Acts of the Apostles. Many of these writings were originally intended to be used in public worship.

The reading of **the Gospel** has always occupied a place of honor in worship. In most churches, the congregation stands during this reading as a sign of respect for Christ, whose life and words the Gospels relate.

The basic form of worship follows a pattern we can trace to the earliest Christians: "They devoted themselves to the apostles' teaching and fellowship, to the breaking of bread and the prayers" (Acts 2:42). We attend to the Word of God, and we share the Meal, Holy Communion.

The liturgy provides a pattern of spoken and sung texts that give flesh to the basic Word/Meal framework. Many parts of the liturgy are from Scripture. While denominations have a variety of traditions, these examples might be familiar to you:

The Greeting, "The grace of our Lord Jesus Christ, the love of God, and the communion of the Holy Spirit be with you all," is from 2 Corinthians 13:14. The verse is the closing of this letter from Paul to the church in Corinth.

The Hymn of Praise, which begins, "Glory to God in the highest," recalls the hymn the angels sang in the fields outside Bethlehem to announce Jesus' birth (Luke 2:14).

After **the offering** has been received, especially when Holy Communion is not celebrated, some congregations sing several verses from Psalm 51: "Create in me a clean heart, O God, and renew a right spirit within me…" (verses 10-12).

The liturgy for Holy Communion incorporates a number of Bible texts. **The Sanctus,** "Holy, holy, holy Lord, God of pow'r and might," sung near the beginning of this portion of the liturgy, is based on Isaiah 6:3. The prophet Isaiah was in the temple and saw a vision of angels, who sang this hymn of praise. (The word *sanctus* is Latin for "holy.")

The Words of Institution ("In the night in which he was betrayed, our Lord Jesus took bread…. Again, after supper, he took the cup…") do not have a single source. The narrative is a composition based on Matthew 26:26-28; Mark 14:22-25; Luke 22:17-20; and 1 Corinthians 11:23-26.

After Communion has been served, the congregation may join in the **hymn of thanks** that a devout, elderly man, Simeon, sang as he cradled the baby Jesus in his arms (Luke 2:29-32).

One customary **benediction,** or blessing, at the end of the service is from Numbers 6:24-27. God commanded Israel's leader, Aaron, to bless the people with words similar to these: "The Lord bless you and keep you. The Lord make his face shine on you and be gracious to you. The Lord look upon you with favor and give you peace."

Some congregations use another benediction, "Almighty God, Father, Son, and Holy Spirit, bless you now and forever." This blessing recalls Jesus' last words to his disciples before he ascended into heaven (Matthew 28:19).

Using These Resources in Other Settings

TODAY'S NORM for scheduling Christian education opportunities involves flexibility and choices. **Bible Basics for Adults** resources have been designed with this in mind. Each course has been designed for use in six sessions that may vary in length from 45 to 60 minutes. Although this structure will work for many adults, the reality is that today's learners have diverse and unpredictable schedules. Therefore, different options must be available to complete a study.

We learn the biblical message and its importance for our lives in a variety of settings. Corporate worship, devotions, class discussions, retreats, and personal conversations represent some of the ways we learn about the Bible. It is therefore valuable to be open to different possibilities that can help adults begin the journey of studying the Bible as part of their Christian life and faith.

Encourage people to participate in the course by providing alternatives to help learners who cannot attend six weekly sessions.

Mentoring

A study group may want to encourage participants to serve as mentors to one another when someone is absent for a particular session. For example, if Sally is unable to attend a session, Juanita, a fellow learner in the class, could meet with or telephone Sally and share some of the key discussions and learning that Juanita recalls from the time the group last met. This way Sally remains connected to the course material, and Juanita enjoys the pleasure of serving a neighbor and reinforcing her own learning at the same time. This experience not only helps Sally and Juanita review biblical material, it also helps Sally remember she is a valued member of the group.

Retreats

Entirely different educational environments can also be explored. A one-day event or an overnight retreat can provide meaningful alternatives to a weekly class schedule. In either case, the course material can be woven together with worship, community building activities, small group work, games, singing, reflection exercises, and more. All of these possibilities can be developed from recommendations in the leader guide and learner book.

Independent Study

Recognizing that not all adults are willing to study in groups nor able to fit into specific class schedules, another educational format could be an independent study that involves a mentor who helps guide the learning process. This way it is easier to find times when people can meet, discuss the sessions, and learn together. A slight variation of this approach would be to give an individual both the leader guide and learner book and allow that person to study independently. It would still be good in this scenario to have two or three meetings with another person to reflect upon the insights, questions, concerns, and commitments that emerge from studying the Bible.

Lifelong Learning

Whatever options are explored to help adults begin the journey of lifelong study of the Bible, a primary goal is to learn about the Bible in the context of a community's nurturing relationships. This reflects the important principle that building and maintaining caring relationships is integral to Christian education. It reminds us that the Holy Spirit works in our lives through others (1 Corinthians 12:7). The benefit of this goal and principle is the experience of growing in faith through the service, insights, support, and modeling of others.

Glossary

Apocalyptic. Writings that report mysterious revelations mediated by angels and disclosing a supernatural world, or that deal with a cataclysmic end of the world.

Disciple. A follower of a public teacher. One of the twelve specially called and instructed by Jesus. Any follower of Jesus.

Doxology. A hymn that expresses praise to God.

Epistle. A letter, specifically those in the New Testament written to congregations or colleagues of the writer.

Evangelist. A person who announces the good news of the gospel. Also, more specifically, a writer of one of the four Gospels.

Exile. The captivity of the Northern Kingdom by the Assyrians in 721 B.C. or the captivity of the Southern Kingdom by the Babylonians in 586 B.C. People of each kingdom were deported to the conquerors' lands.

Exodus. The departure of the Israelites under the leadership of Moses from slavery in Egypt.

Faith. A trusting relationship with God.

Gentiles. Those people who are not Jews.

Gospel. Good news; preached by Jesus or about Jesus. New Testament books (Matthew, Mark, Luke, John) that contain the story of Jesus' life.

Grace. The unmerited and abundant gift of God's love and favor through Christ.

Greek. In the Bible, Greek refers to those who were not Jews or people who lived under Roman rule. The 27 books of the New Testament were written in the ancient language of Greek.

Hebrew. Original language of most of the Old Testament

Hebrews. People of Israel, descendants of Abraham.

Litany. A prayer consisting of a series of petitions offered by a leader, alternating with responses from the congregation.

Martin Luther. A medieval (1483–1546) professor of theology who inspired a reformation of the church based on the scriptural principle that we are "saved by grace through faith" (Ephesians 2:8).

Parable. A method of speech in which a moral or religious truth is illustrated by analogy with common experience. Jesus often taught through parables.

Promised Land. The land of Canaan that God gave the Israelites after their exodus from Egypt and 40 years' wandering in the wilderness of the Sinai peninsula.

Prophet. An authoritative and infallible teacher who speaks God's word, especially words of judgment, at God's command.

Rabbi. Master, teacher in the Jewish faith.

Reconciliation. Making peace, making friends with.

Repentance. Feeling regret, admitting one's sinfulness, and beginning a new life.

Theology. Study of God and God's relationship to the world.

Session 1
Exodus
Grace
Greek
Hebrew
Hebrews
Martin Luther
Promised Land
Rabbi

Session 2
Exile
Prophet
Repentance

Session 3
Epistle
Evangelist
Grace
Reconciliation

Session 4
Disciple
Epistle
Faith
Gentiles
Hebrews
Parable
Theology

Session 5
Apocalyptic
Doxology
Gospel
Grace
Litany